Thanks Be To God

Thanksgiving and Autumn

King James Version

Bible Cursive Practice
Activity Book for Kids

with Connect the Dots, Coloring, Drawing, Mazes, and More!

This Book Belongs To:

_____

- -

_____

Cursive Trace & Practice

But I will sacrifice

unto thee with the

voice of thanksgiving;

I will pay that

that I have vowed.

Salvation is of the

Lord. Jonah 2:9

Cursive Trace & Practice

Happy Thanksgiving!

Cursive Trace & Practice

I thank thee, and
praise thee, O thou
God of my fathers,
who hast given me
wisdom and might.
Daniel 2:23a

Cursive Trace & Practice

Words from the First Thanksgiving

```
I  Y  W  Q  Z  I  B  M  Z  T  W  D  X  A  V  C  D
Y  Q  U  V  N  P  R  L  T  M  K  M  V  Z  P  Z  G
C  N  E  F  A  Q  Q  G  E  R  Y  W  S  F  N  W  P
K  S  N  R  T  N  T  Z  E  S  K  T  Y  O  X  U  V
O  L  U  G  I  H  M  P  H  S  S  W  S  D  E  N  T
Q  O  Y  M  V  X  A  S  N  I  Q  I  L  Z  Q  H  X
A  I  J  L  E  B  Y  N  N  A  N  U  N  F  Q  W  V
F  O  J  O  S  O  F  O  K  E  Q  A  A  G  R  A  I
E  S  A  J  C  D  L  R  V  S  I  S  C  S  S  M  P
A  A  N  T  K  O  O  Y  R  S  G  T  M  O  H  P  W
S  M  Y  W  C  V  W  R  H  V  P  I  M  Q  R  A  Y
T  E  S  Z  G  G  E  R  N  A  R  Z  V  D  S  N  B
T  R  N  W  T  Y  R  R  S  G  R  O  T  I  N  O  S
F  I  F  B  A  I  O  L  L  O  I  V  R  X  N  A  X
S  C  I  R  O  C  O  I  C  D  W  H  E  A  T  G  J
Z  A  P  Y  T  E  P  U  R  I  T  A  N  S  S  H  J
A  B  G  S  X  B  M  J  Q  V  E  D  I  X  T  X  K
```

GOD	CORN	WHEAT
FEAST	SQUASH	PRAYER
ACORNS	NATIVES	HARVEST
AMERICA	VENISON	PILGRIMS
PURITANS	MAYFLOWER	COLONISTS
WAMPANOAG	BLESSINGS	THANKSGIVING

Now therefore, our

God, we thank thee,

and praise thy

glorious name.

1 Chronicles 29:13

Cursive Trace & Practice

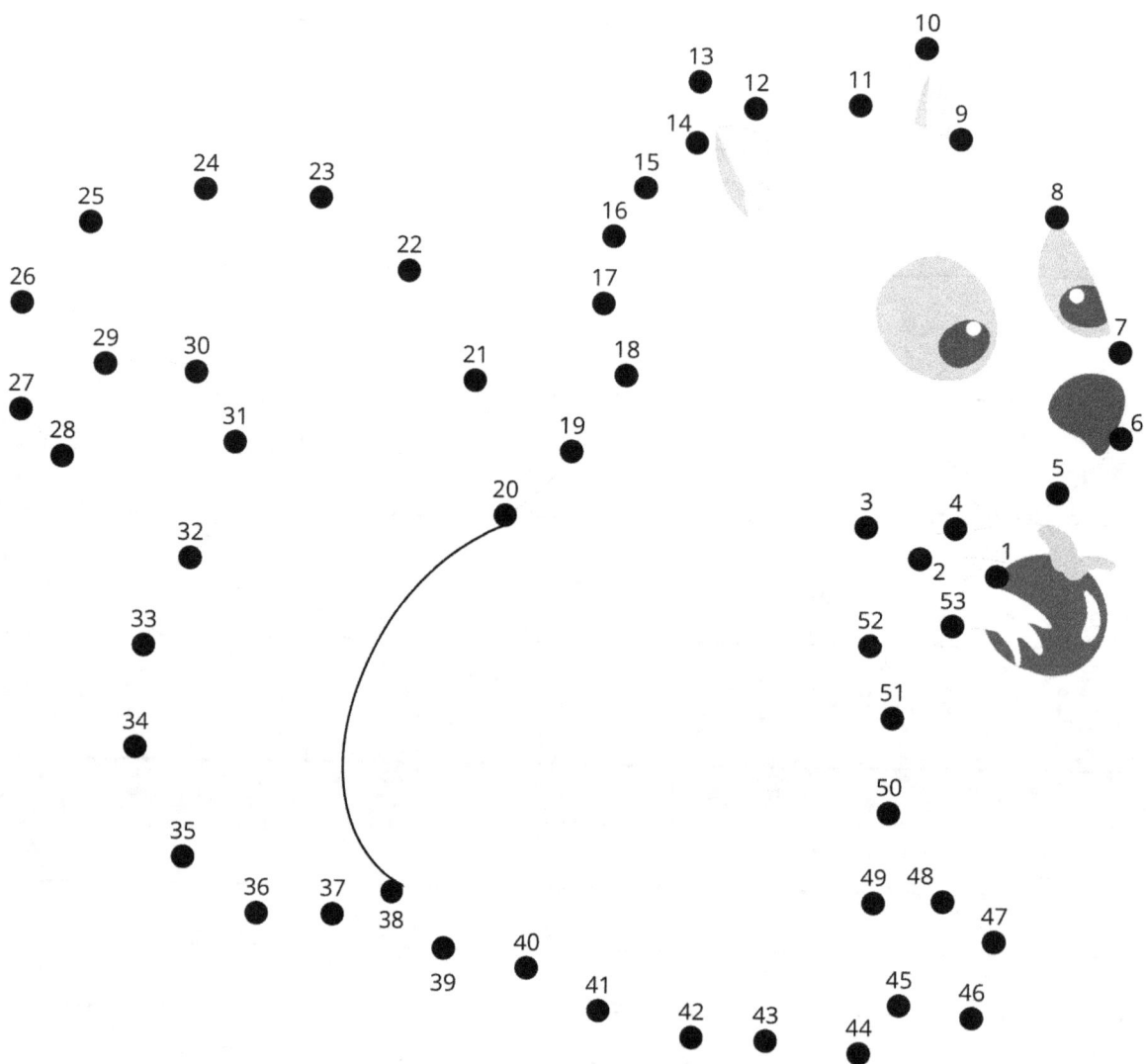

Cursive Trace & Practice

Offer unto God

thanksgiving; and

pay thy vows unto

the most High.

Psalms 50:14

Cursive Trace & Practice

Learn to Draw

Complete the picture by copying what is in each square. One is done as an example.

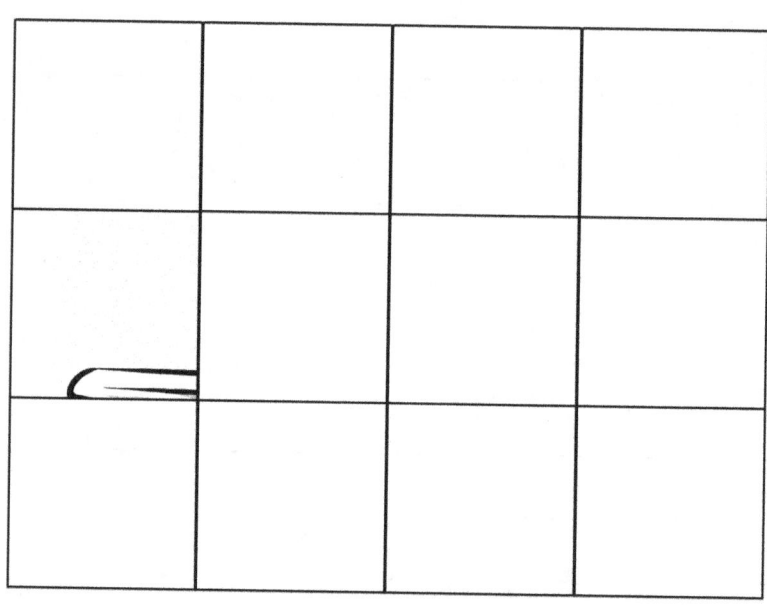

Cursive Trace & Practice

Giving thanks

always for all

things unto God and

the Father in the

name of our Lord

Jesus Christ.

Ephesians 5:20

Cursive Trace & Practice

Help the bees find their hive.

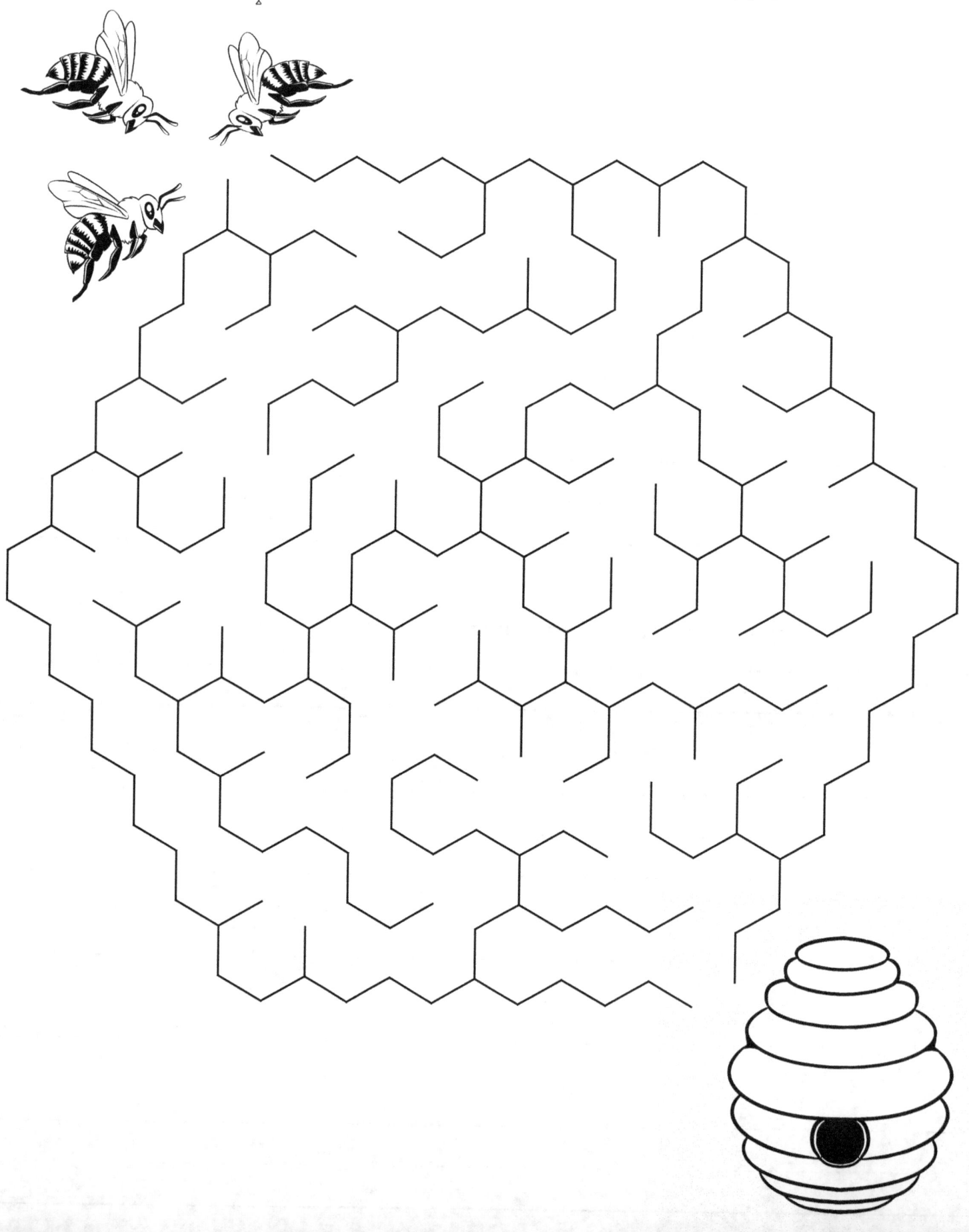

Harvest Time

I will give thee

thanks in the great

congregation: I

will praise thee

among much

people.

Psalms 35:18

Cursive Trace & Practice

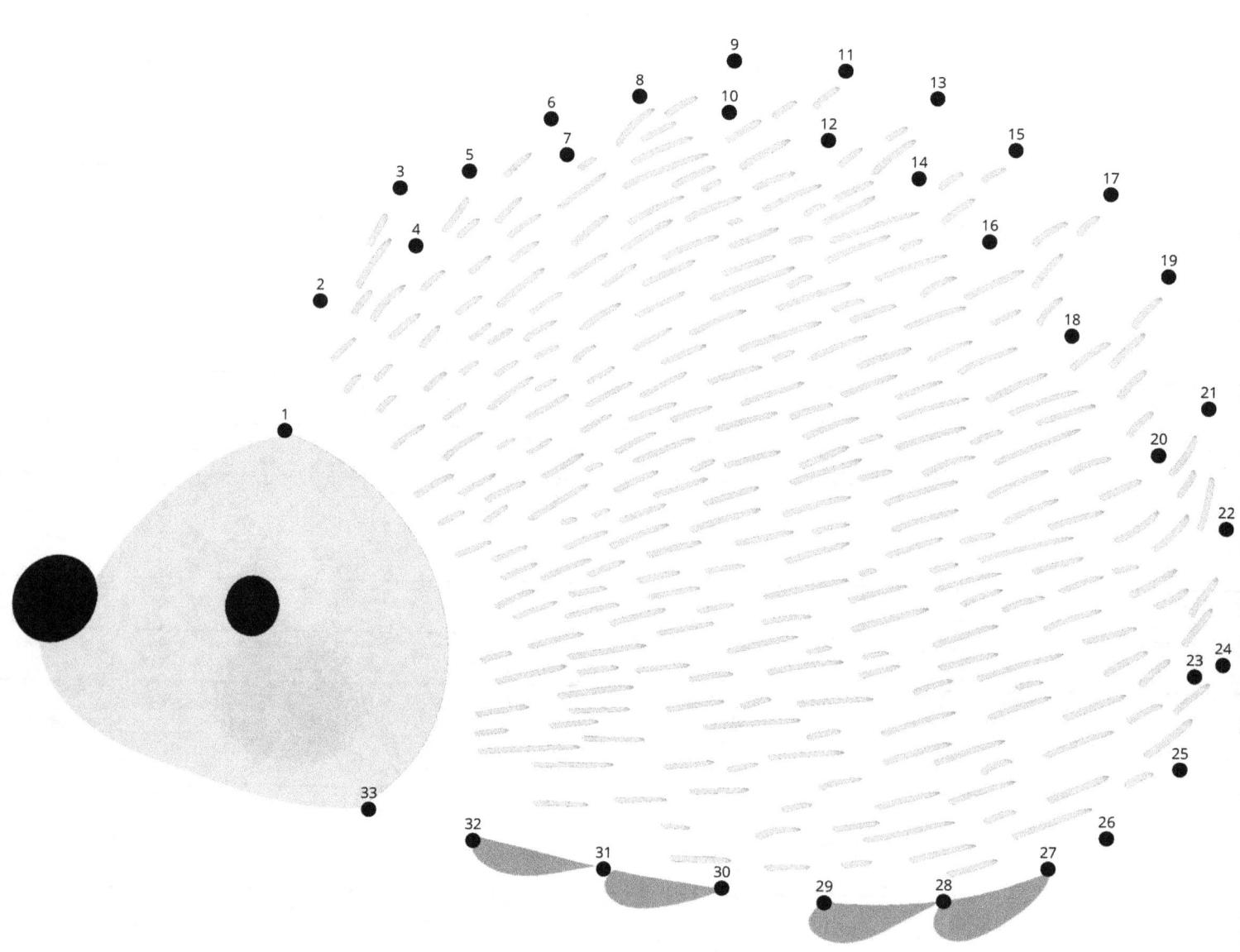

In every thing give

thanks: for this is

the will of God in

Christ Jesus

concerning you.

1 Thessalonians 5:18

Cursive Trace & Practice

Corn Maze

ENTER

EXIT

Cornucopia or
Horn of Plenty

GENESIS 1:11

AND GOD SAID, LET THE EARTH BRING FORTH GRASS,
THE HERB YIELDING SEED, AND THE FRUIT TREE
YIELDING FRUIT AFTER HIS KIND, WHOSE SEED IS IN
ITSELF, UPON THE EARTH: AND IT WAS SO.

Cursive Trace & Practice

Sing unto the Lord,

O ye saints of his,

and give thanks at

the remembrance of

his holiness.

Psalm 30:4

Cursive Trace & Practice

Draw Your Own Leaves on the Tree

SING, O YE HEAVENS; FOR THE LORD HATH DONE IT: SHOUT, YE LOWER PARTS OF THE
EARTH: BREAK FORTH INTO SINGING, YE MOUNTAINS, O FOREST, AND EVERY TREE THEREIN:
FOR THE LORD HATH REDEEMED JACOB, AND GLORIFIED HIMSELF IN ISRAEL. ISAIAH 44:23

Cursive Trace & Practice

Praise ye the Lord.

O give thanks unto

the Lord; for he is

good: for his mercy

endureth for ever.

Psalm 106:1

Cursive Trace & Practice

Help the owl fly to the branch.

But thanks be to

God, which giveth

as the victory

through our Lord

Jesus Christ.

1 Corinthians 15:57

Cursive Trace & Practice

Learn to Draw

Complete the picture by copying what is in each square. One is done as an example.

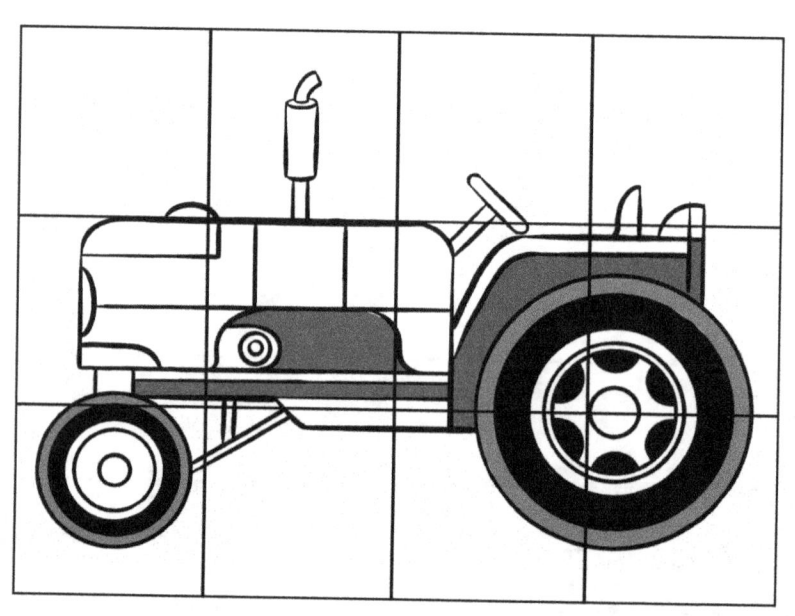

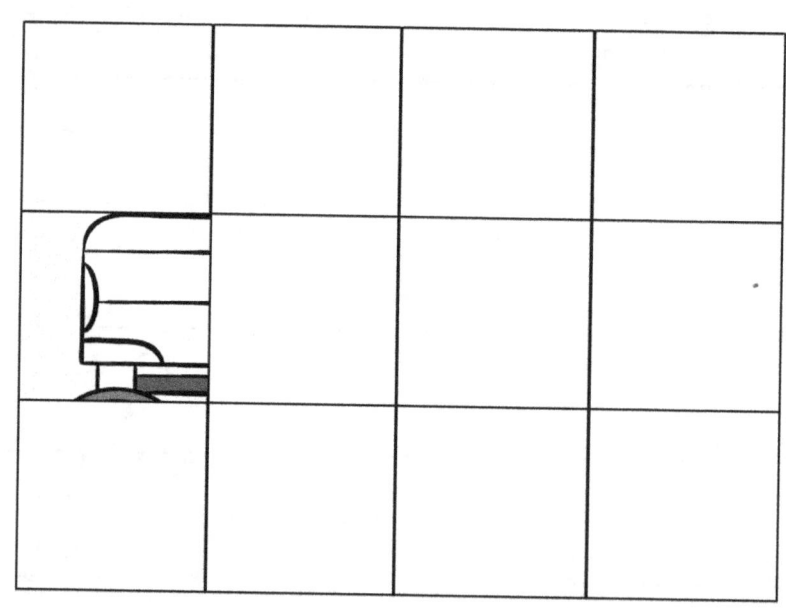

Cursive Trace & Practice

Now thanks be unto

God, which always

causeth us to

triumph in Christ.

2 Corinthians 2:14a

Cursive Trace & Practice

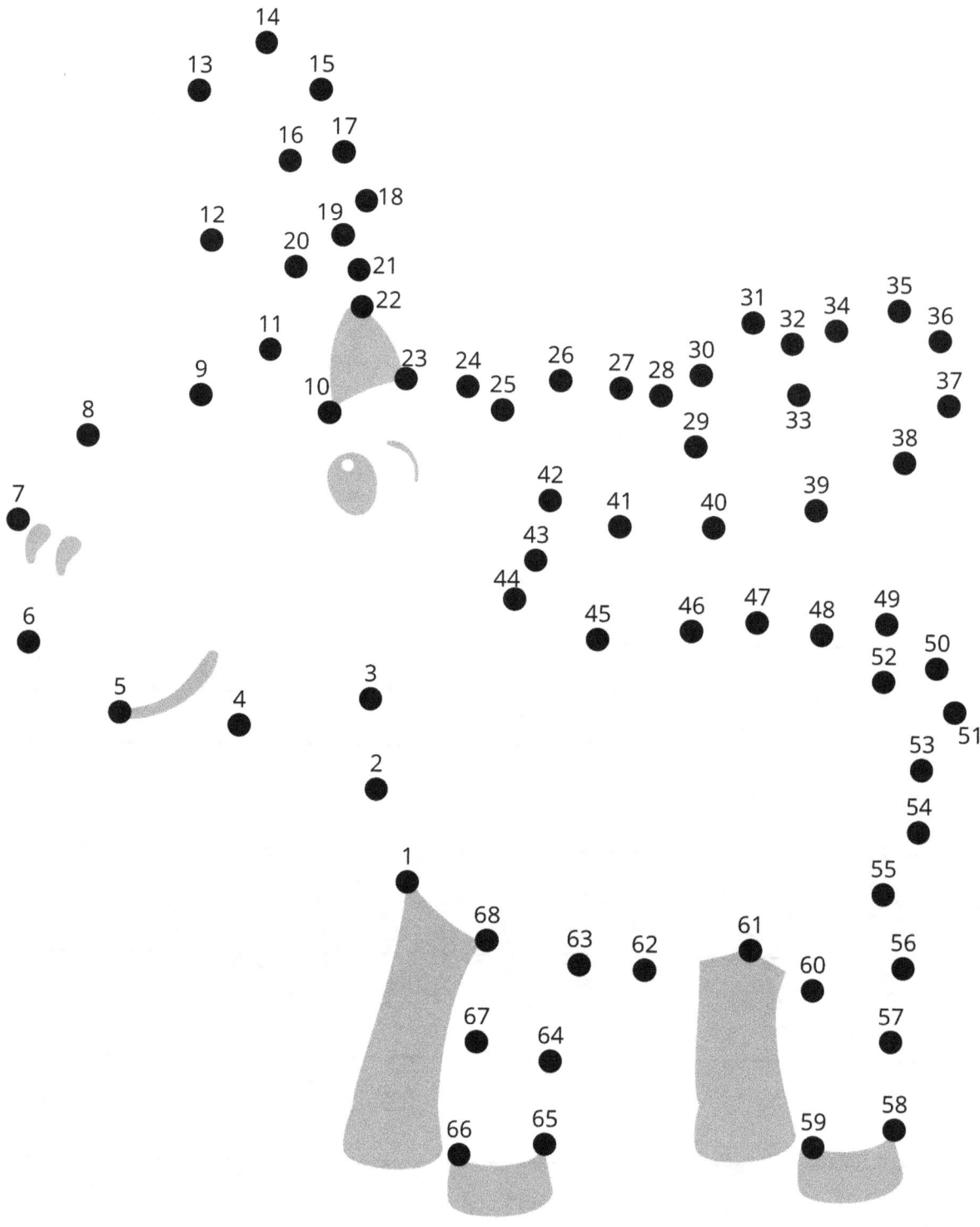

Unto thee, O God,

do we give thanks,

unto thee do we

give thanks: for

that thy name is

near thy wondrous

works declare.

Psalms 75:1

Cursive Trace & Practice

Learn to Draw

Complete the picture by copying what is in
each square. One is done as an example.

Cursive Trace & Practice

It is a good thing

to give thanks unto

the Lord, and to

sing praises unto

thy name, O Most

High. Psalm 92:1

Cursive Trace & Practice

Help the opossum get to the trees.

Cursive Trace & Practice

O give thanks unto

the Lord; call

upon his name:

make known his

deeds among the

people. Psalms 105:1

Cursive Trace & Practice

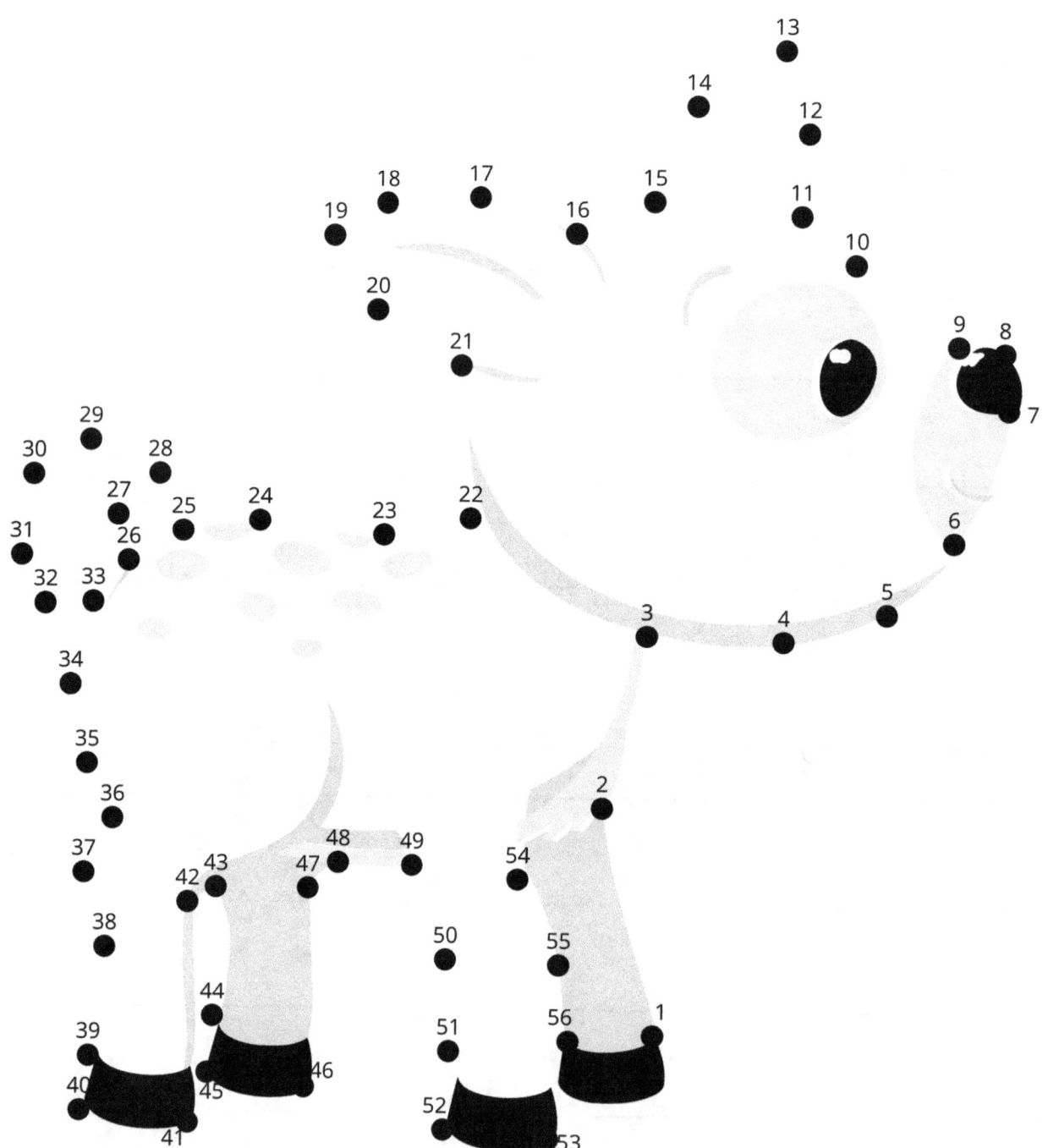

Cursive Trace & Practice

I will offer to thee

the sacrifice of

thanksgiving, and

will call upon the

name of the Lord.

Psalms 116:17

Cursive Trace & Practice

Learn to Draw

Complete the picture by copying what is in each square. One is done as an example.

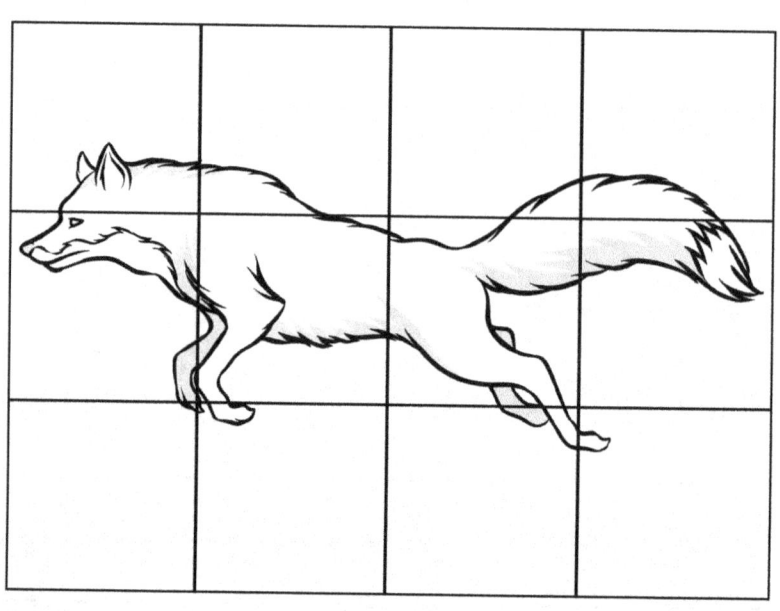

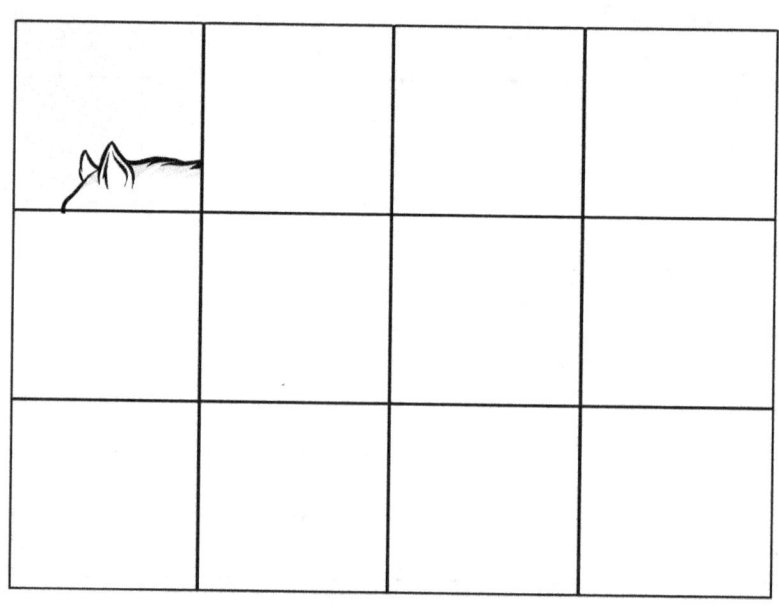

I will praise the

name of God with a

song, and will

magnify him with

thanksgiving.

Psalms 69:30

Cursive Trace & Practice

Thanksgiving Menu

```
A  S  C  T  U  R  K  E  Y  V  R  B  U  P
P  Q  W  E  O  C  S  V  M  O  K  W  V  D
P  U  C  R  P  O  T  A  T  O  E  S  R  J
L  A  M  M  K  R  U  P  L  B  P  E  A  S
E  S  A  P  C  N  F  T  U  A  T  B  Z  U
D  H  O  P  K  J  F  Z  J  T  D  R  G  J
N  R  K  Y  K  I  I  F  U  Y  G  F  K  H
R  D  E  C  R  A  N  B  E  R  R  Y  B  M
A  O  P  S  R  W  G  Q  E  J  J  T  J  W
U  P  L  E  S  M  P  R  Y  U  M  Q  V  Y
Y  L  D  L  C  I  K  O  A  R  T  U  P  K
M  I  N  I  S  A  N  V  M  V  Z  K  I  K
C  H  M  N  G  C  N  G  S  P  Y  B  I  X
D  E  Y  L  G  F  X  B  A  G  B  M  W  O
```

APPLE	GRAVY	ROLLS
BUTTER	HAM	SALAD
CIDER	PEAS	SQUASH
CORN	PECAN	STUFFING
CRANBERRY	POTATOES	TURKEY
DRESSING	PUMPKIN	YAMS

Mirror Image

Complete the picture by drawing the mirror image of what is in each square. One is done as an example.

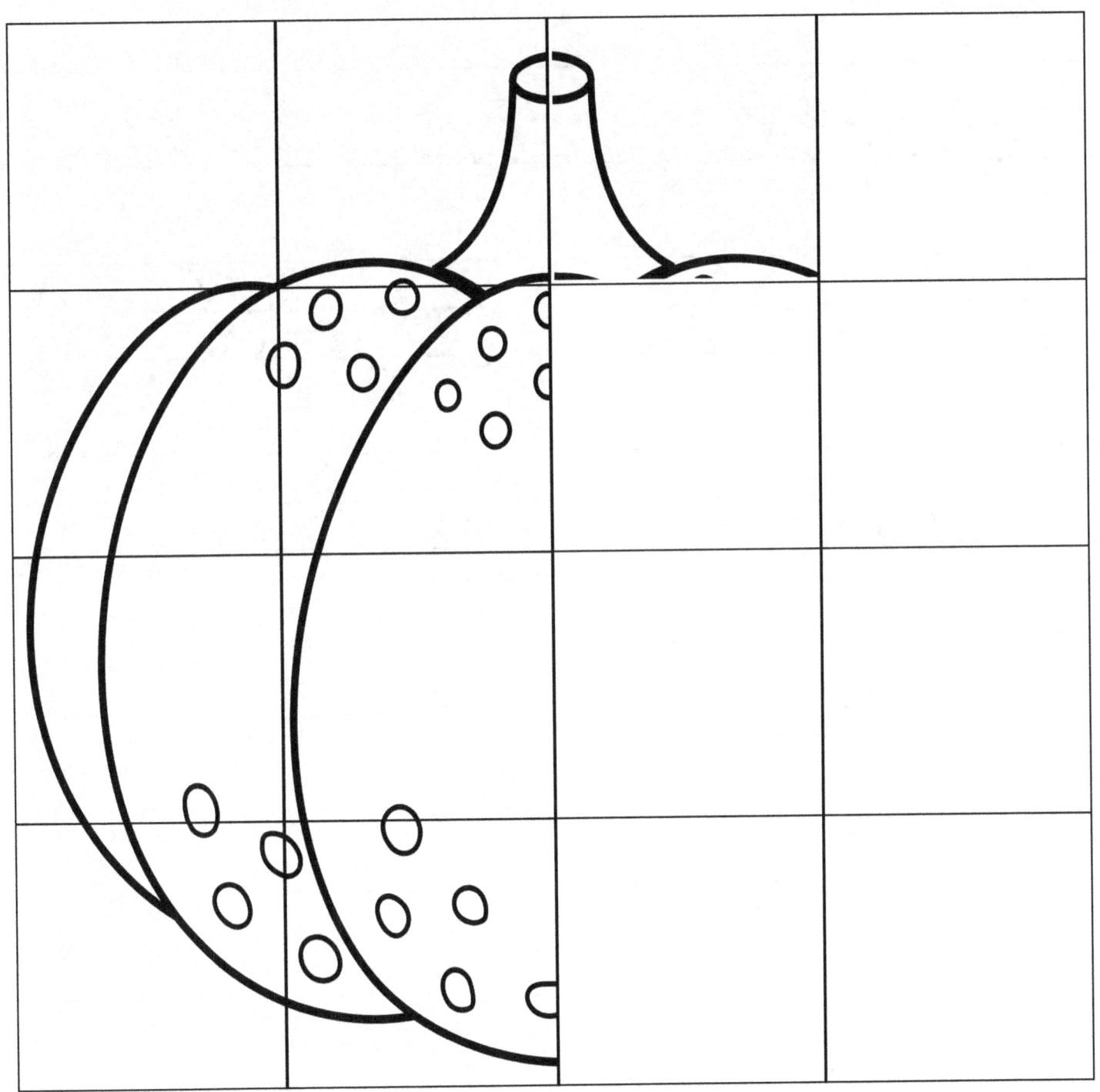

Let us come before

his presence with

thanksgiving, and

make a joyful

noise unto him

with psalms.

Psalms 95:2

Cursive Trace & Practice

Help the skunk find his hole under the log.

Cursive Trace & Practice

And let the peace of
God rule in your
hearts, to the which
also ye are called in
one body; and be
ye thankful.
Colossians 3:15

Cursive Trace & Practice

Learn to Draw

Complete the picture by copying what is in each square. One is done as an example.

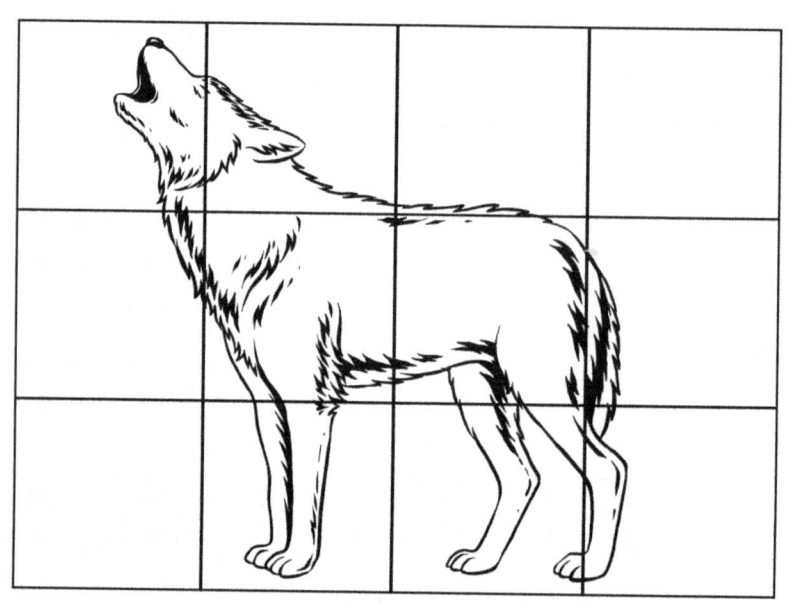

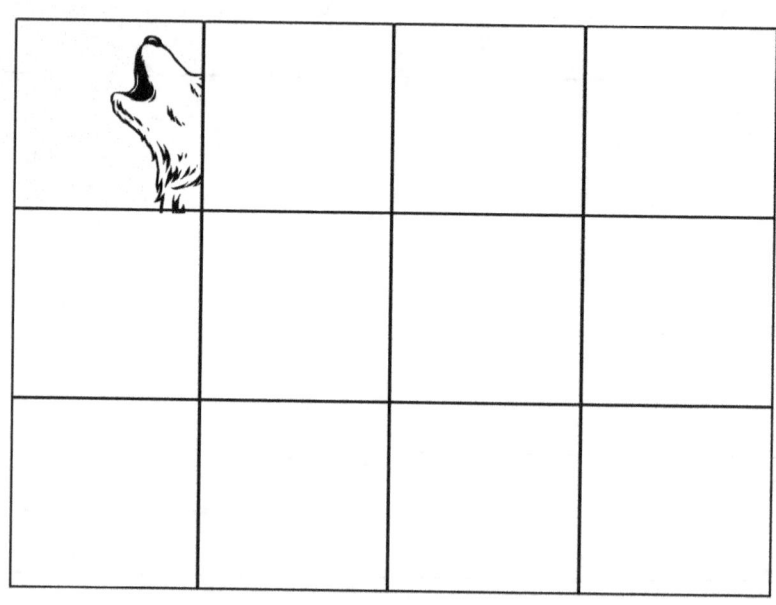

Cursive Trace & Practice

And whatsoever ye
do in word or deed,
do all in the name
of the Lord Jesus,
giving thanks to God
and the Father by
him. Colossians 3:17

Cursive Trace & Practice

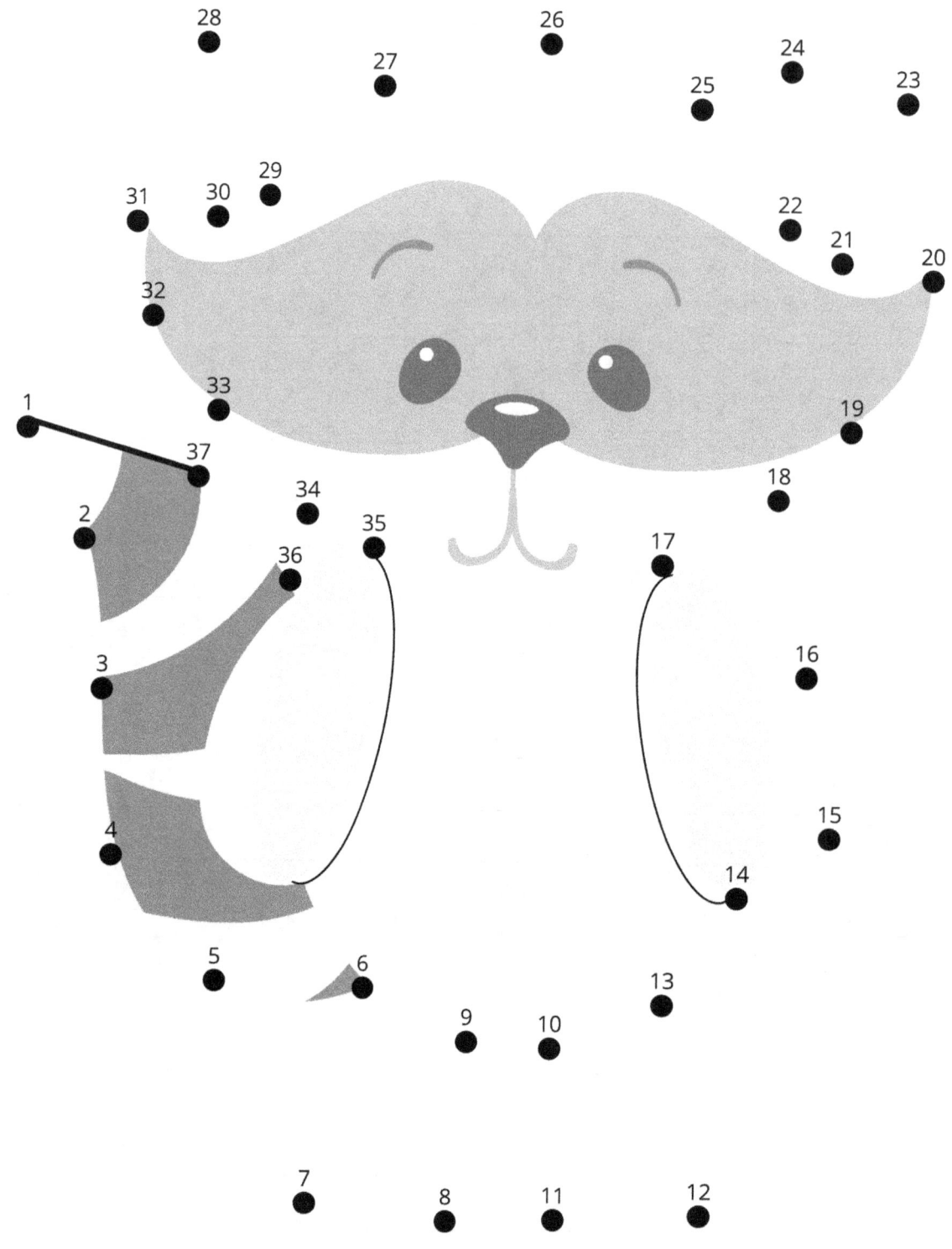

Mirror Image

Complete the picture by drawing the mirror image of what is in each square. One is done as an example.

By him therefore let

us offer the sacrifice

of praise to God

continually, that is,

the fruit of our

lips giving thanks

to his name.

Hebrews 13:15

Cursive Trace & Practice

Mirror Image

Complete the picture by drawing the mirror image of what is in each square. One is done as an example.

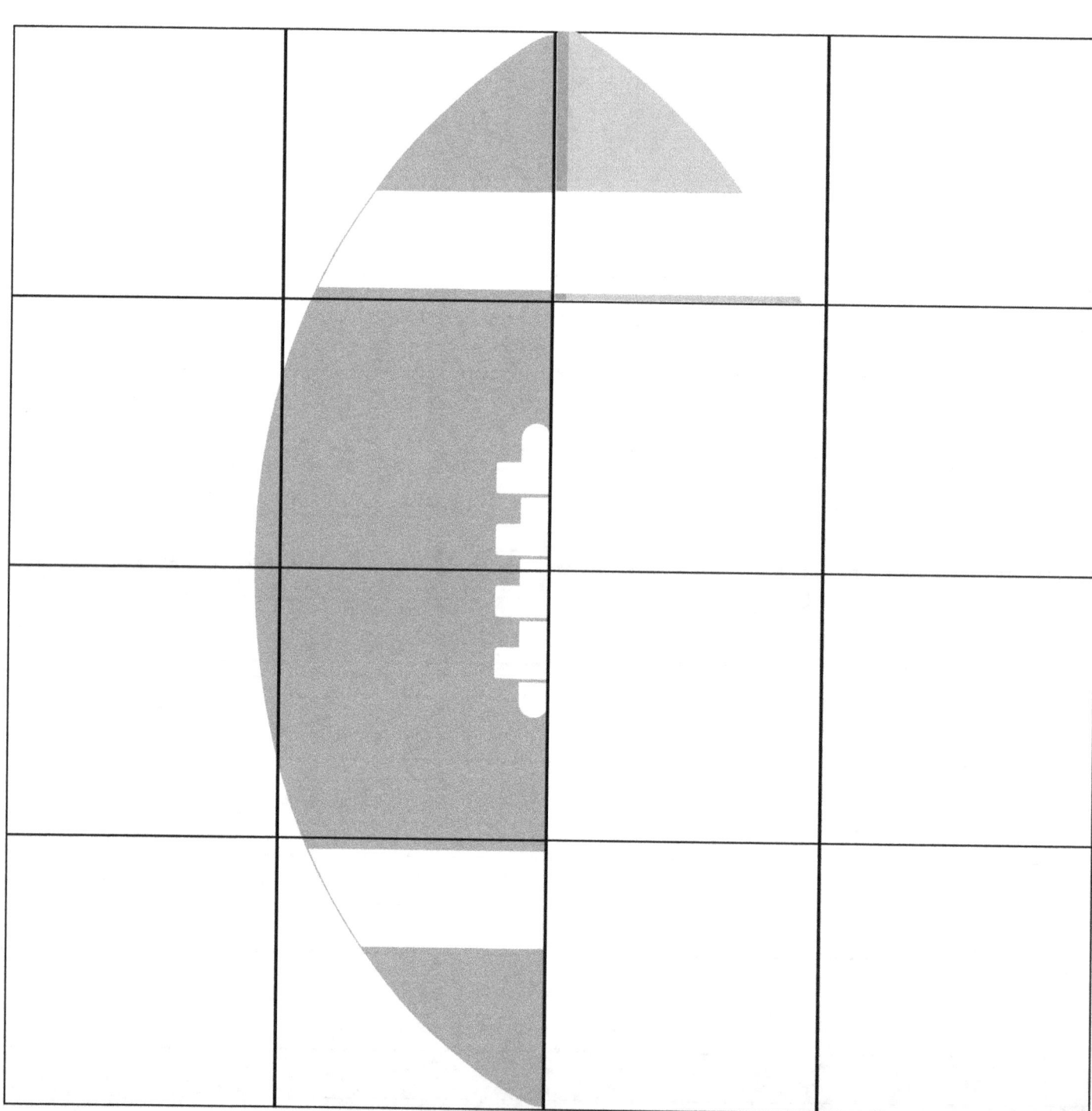

Farm Market

Corn Maze Solution

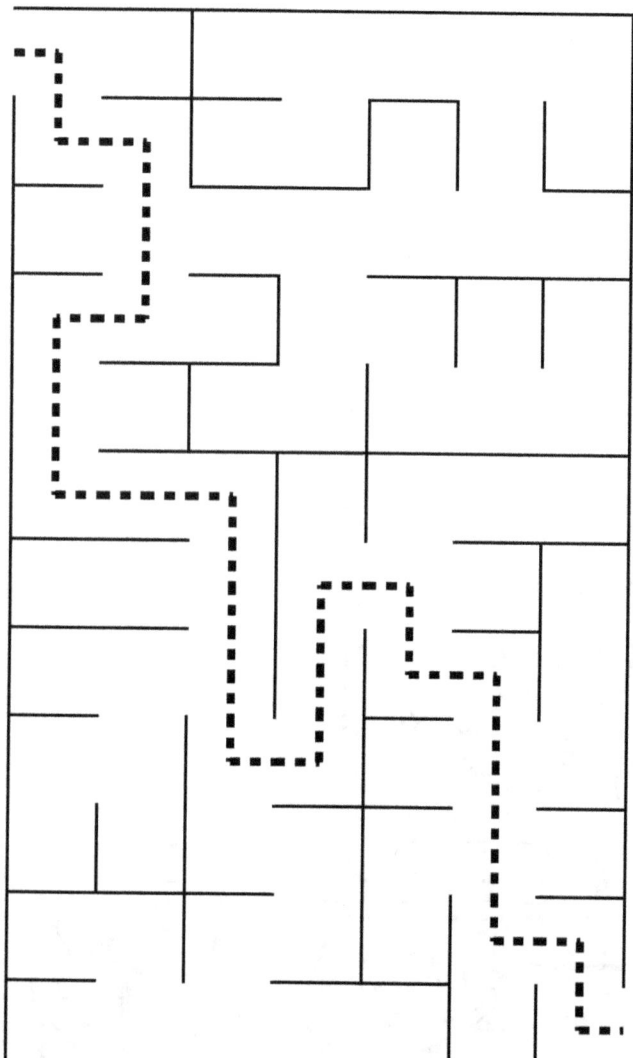

Thanksgiving Menu Word Search

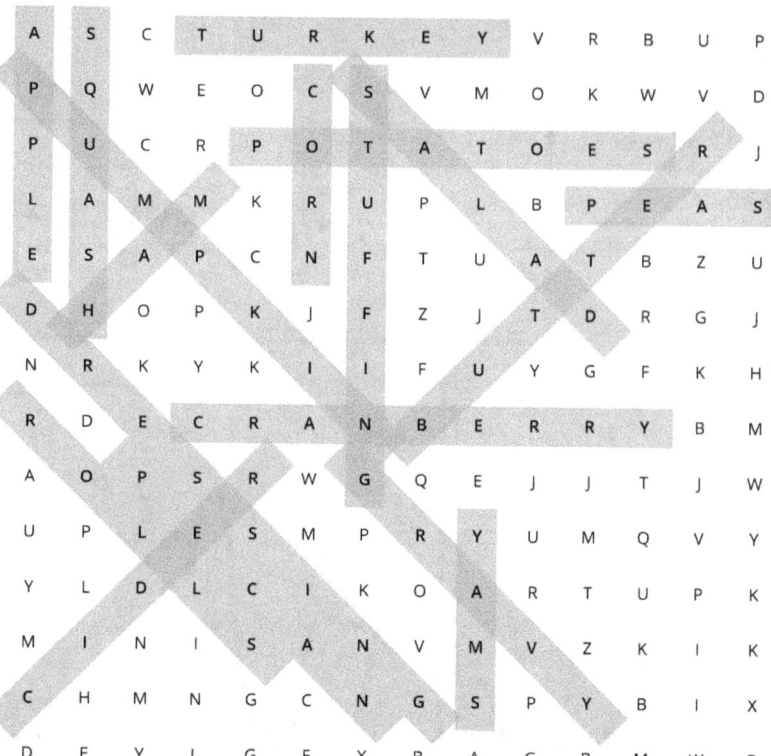

A	S	C	T	U	R	K	E	Y	V	R	B	U	P
P	Q	W	E	O	C	S	V	M	O	K	W	V	D
P	U	C	R	P	O	T	A	T	O	E	S	R	J
L	A	M	M	K	R	U	P	L	B	P	E	A	S
E	S	A	P	C	N	F	T	U	A	T	B	Z	U
D	H	O	P	K	J	F	Z	J	T	D	R	G	J
N	R	K	Y	K	I	I	F	U	Y	G	F	K	H
R	D	E	C	R	A	N	B	E	R	R	Y	B	M
A	O	P	S	R	W	G	Q	E	J	J	T	J	W
U	P	L	E	S	M	P	R	Y	U	M	Q	V	Y
Y	L	D	L	C	I	K	O	A	R	T	U	P	K
M	I	N	I	S	A	N	V	M	V	Z	K	I	K
C	H	M	N	G	C	N	G	S	P	Y	B	I	X
D	E	Y	L	G	F	X	B	A	G	B	M	W	O

First Thanksgiving Word Search

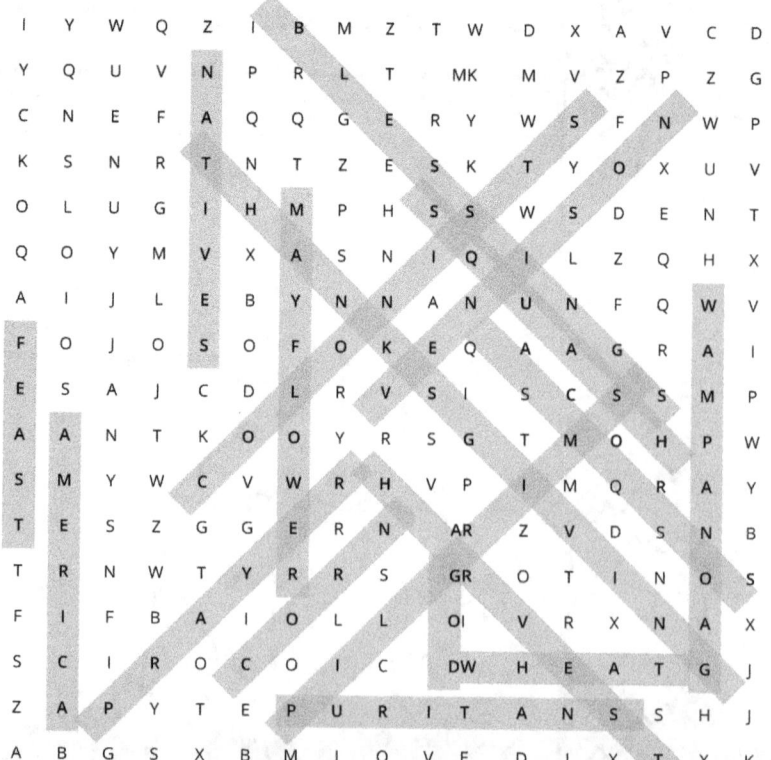

I	Y	W	Q	Z	I	B	M	Z	T	W	D	X	A	V	C	D
Y	Q	U	V	N	P	R	L	T	MK	M	V	Z	P	Z	G
C	N	E	F	A	Q	Q	G	E	R	Y	W	S	F	N	W	P
K	S	N	R	T	N	T	Z	E	S	K	T	Y	O	X	U	V
O	L	U	G	I	H	M	P	H	S	S	W	S	D	E	N	T
Q	O	Y	M	V	A	A	S	N	I	Q	I	L	Z	Q	H	X
A	I	J	L	E	B	Y	N	N	A	N	U	N	F	Q	W	V
F	O	J	O	S	O	F	O	K	E	Q	A	A	G	R	A	I
E	S	A	J	C	D	L	R	V	S	I	S	C	S	S	M	P
A	A	N	T	K	O	O	Y	R	S	G	T	M	O	H	P	W
M	M	Y	W	C	V	W	R	H	V	P	I	M	Q	R	A	Y
T	E	S	Z	G	G	E	R	N	AR	Z	V	D	S	N	B
T	R	N	W	T	Y	R	R	S	GR	O	T	I	N	O	S
F	I	F	B	A	I	O	L	L	O	I	V	R	X	N	A	X
S	C	I	R	O	C	O	I	C	DW	H	E	A	T	G	J
Z	A	P	Y	T	E	P	U	R	I	T	A	N	S	S	H	J
A	B	G	S	X	B	M	J	Q	V	E	D	I	X	T	X	K

Skunk Maze Solution

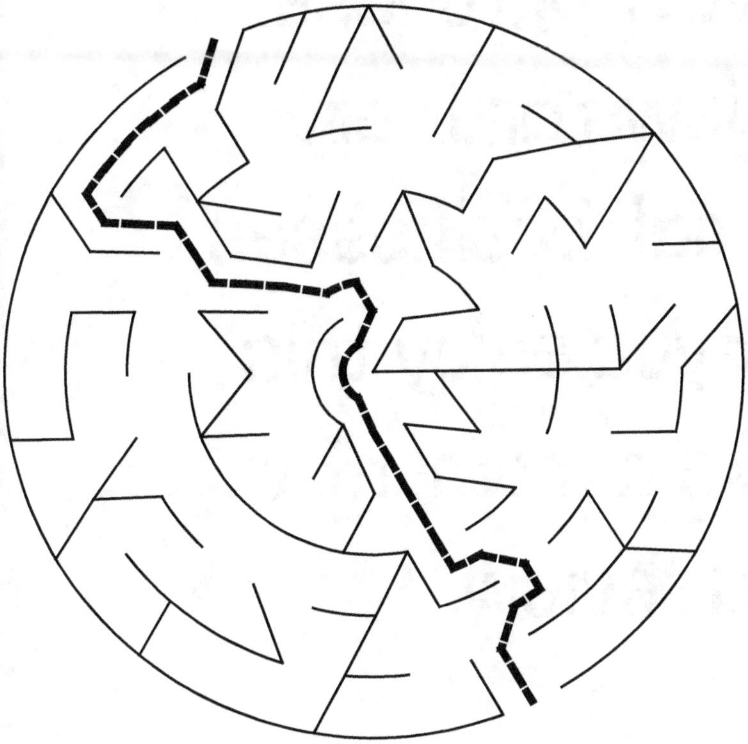

Bees Maze Solution

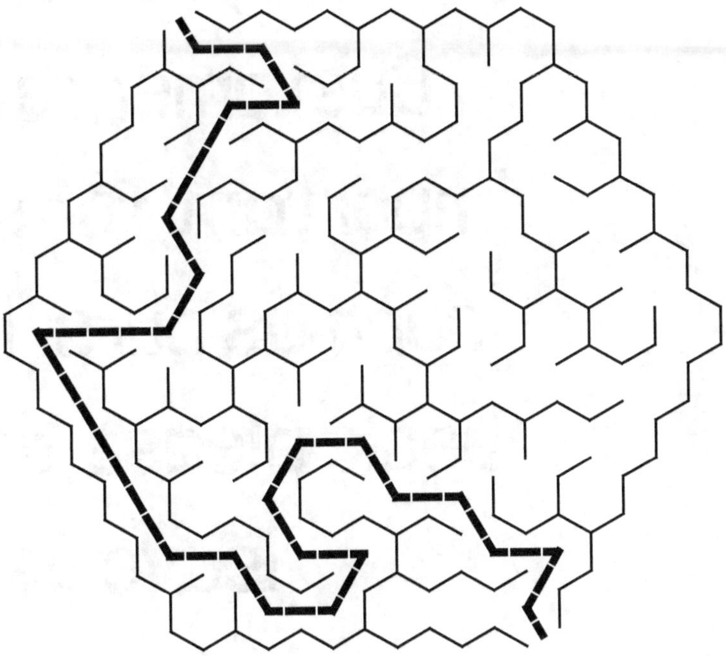

Owl Maze Solution

Opossum Maze Solution

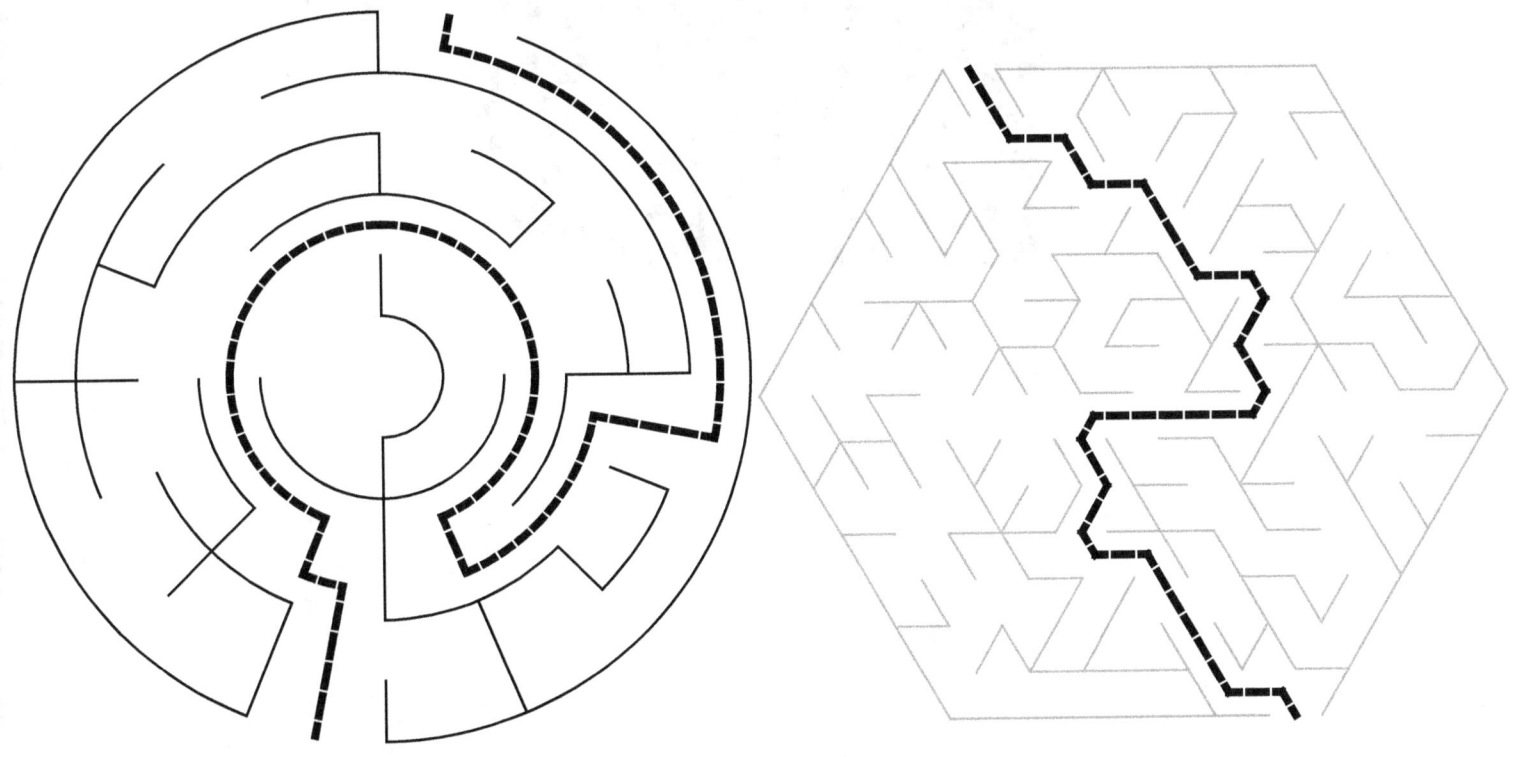

Thank you for your purchase!
Customer reviews are very
important for small businesses
such as ours. If you enjoy this
book, please take a moment to
leave us a review.